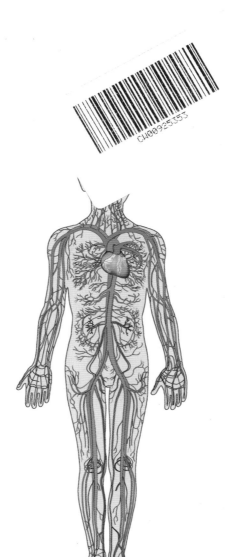

Note to parents, carers and teachers

Read it yourself is a series of modern stories, favourite characters, traditional tales and first reference books, written in a simple way for children who are learning to read. The books can be read independently or as part of a guided reading session.

Each book is carefully structured to include many high-frequency words vital for first reading. The sentences on each page are supported closely by pictures to help with understanding, and to offer lively details to talk about.

The books are graded into four levels that progressively introduce wider vocabulary and longer text as a reader's ability and confidence grows.

Ideas for use

- Although your child will now be progressing towards silent, independent reading, let her know that your help and encouragement is always available.

- Developing readers can be concentrating so hard on the words that they sometimes don't fully grasp the meaning of what they're reading. Answering the quiz questions at the end of the book will help with understanding.

For more information and advice on Read it yourself and book banding, visit **www.ladybird.com/readityourself**

Book
Band
10

Level 4 is ideal for children who are ready to read longer stories with a wider vocabulary and are eager to start reading independently.

Special features:

Detailed illustrations capture the imagination

Full exploration of subject

Richer, more varied vocabulary

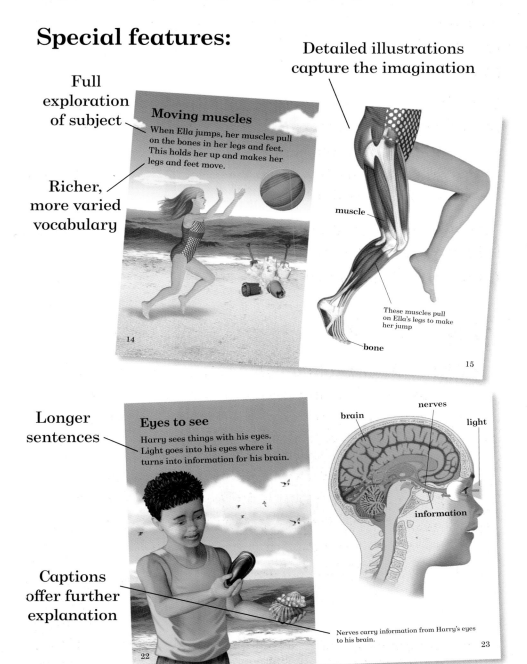

Moving muscles

When Ella jumps, her muscles pull on the bones in her legs and feet. This holds her up and makes her legs and feet move.

muscle

These muscles pull on Ella's legs to make her jump

bone

14

15

Longer sentences

Eyes to see

Harry sees things with his eyes. Light goes into his eyes where it turns into information for his brain.

Captions offer further explanation

brain

nerves

light

information

Nerves carry information from Harry's eyes to his brain.

22

23

Educational Consultant: Geraldine Taylor
Book Banding Consultant: Kate Ruttle
Subject Consultant: Dr Kim Dennis-Bryan

LADYBIRD BOOKS

UK | USA | Canada | Ireland | Australia
India | New Zealand | South Africa

Ladybird Books is part of the Penguin Random House group of companies
whose addresses can be found at global.penguinrandomhouse.com.

ladybird.com

Penguin
Random House
UK

First published 2016
001

Printed in China

A CIP catalogue record for this book is available from the British Library

ISBN: 978–0–24123–767–0

The Human Body

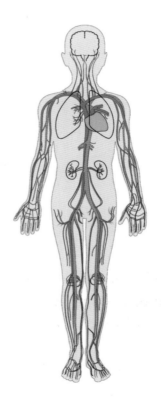

Written by Chris Baker
Illustrated by Laszlo Veres

Contents

Busy bodies

Harry and Ella like to play ball.
They use many parts of their
bodies when they play.

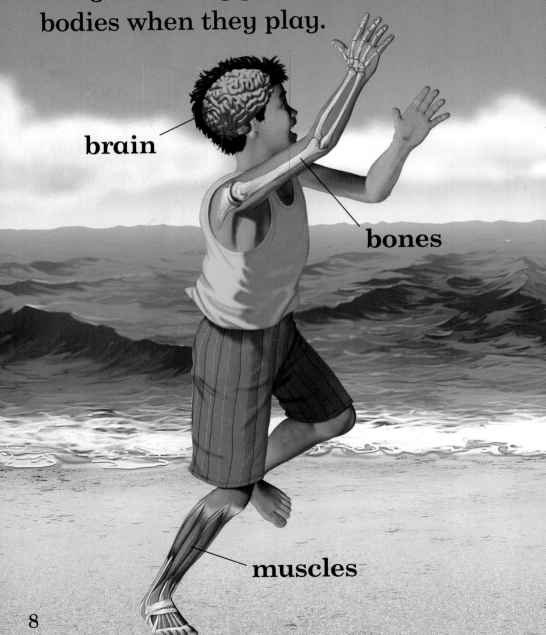

brain

bones

muscles

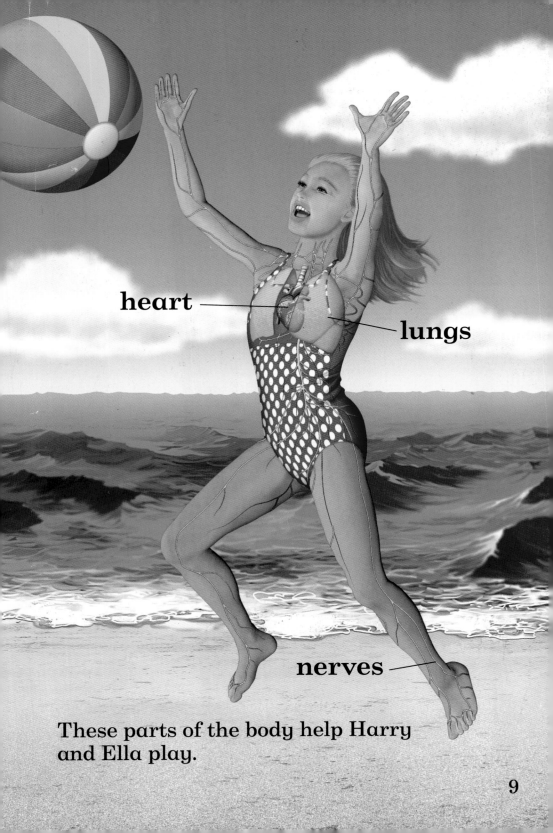

heart

lungs

nerves

These parts of the body help Harry and Ella play.

Skeleton bones

Bones are hard and strong. They work with our muscles to hold our bodies up.

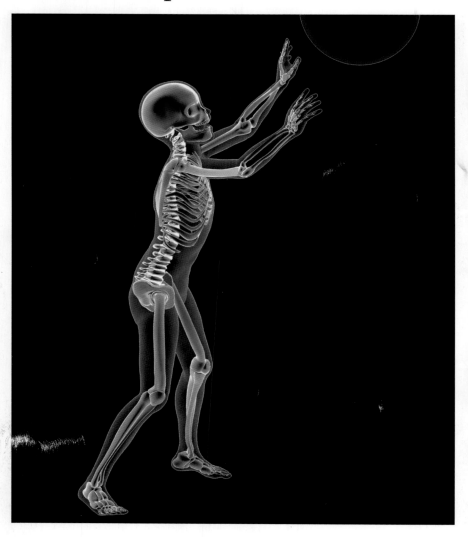

Together, Harry's bones make a skeleton.

Our hard, strong bones also protect
the other body parts.

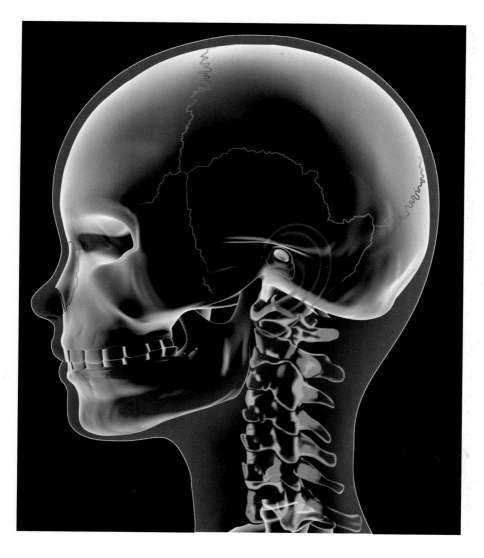

Bones protect Ella's brain here.

Muscles and bones

Bones and muscles work together to help Harry and Ella move. Muscles pull on bones to make them move.

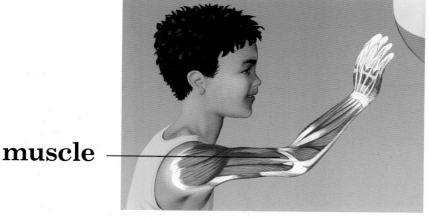

muscle

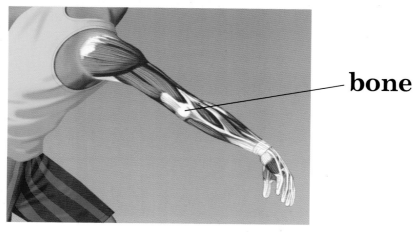

bone

Harry's muscles have to pull back the bones in his arm to make his arm move.

Moving muscles

When Ella jumps, her muscles pull on the bones in her legs and feet. This holds her up and makes her legs and feet move.

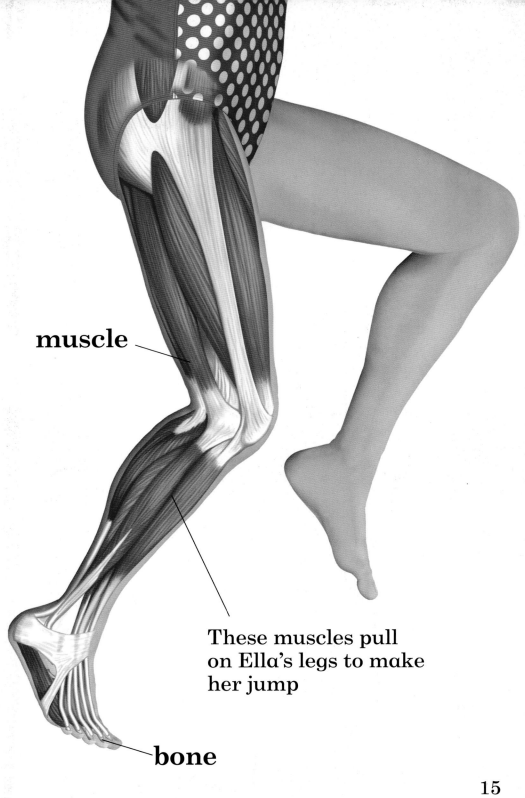

muscle

bone

These muscles pull
on Ella's legs to make
her jump

Amazing brains

Ella and Harry's brains are the control centres for their bodies.

From the control centre of Ella's brain, nerves have to carry orders down to Ella's muscles so that Ella can jump.

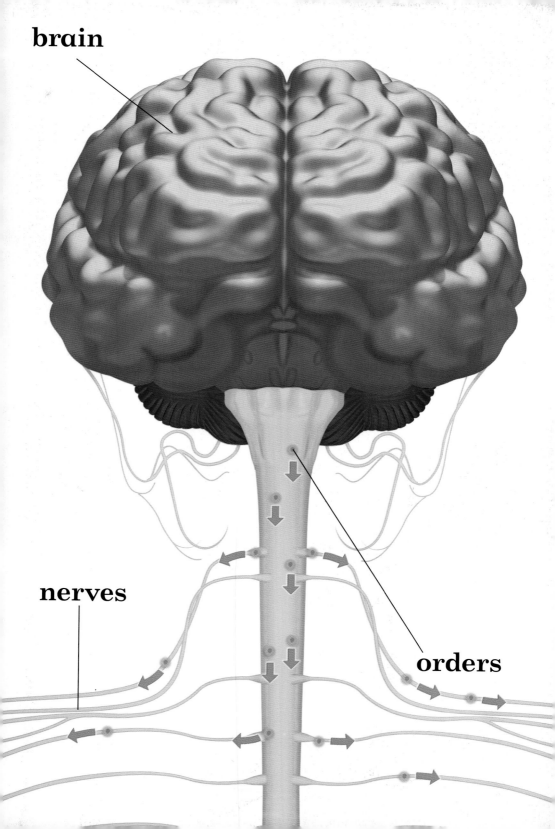

brain

nerves

orders

Brain and nerves

Other nerves carry information back to Ella's brain. Then her brain uses the new information to make the next orders.

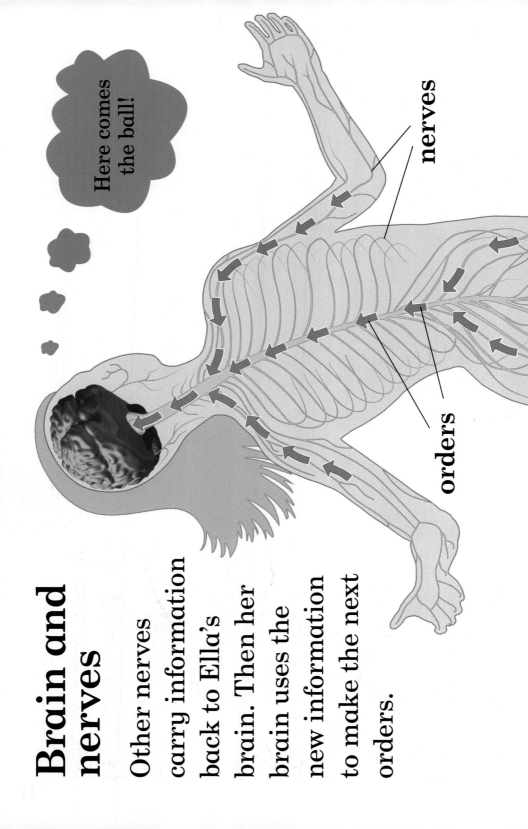

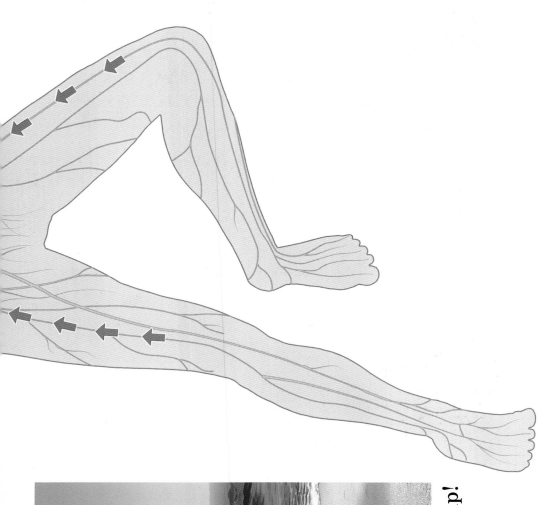

Now Ella needs to jump!

Brain game

We also use our brains to think
and remember. Ella's brain thinks
she would like this game, and
remembers how to play it.

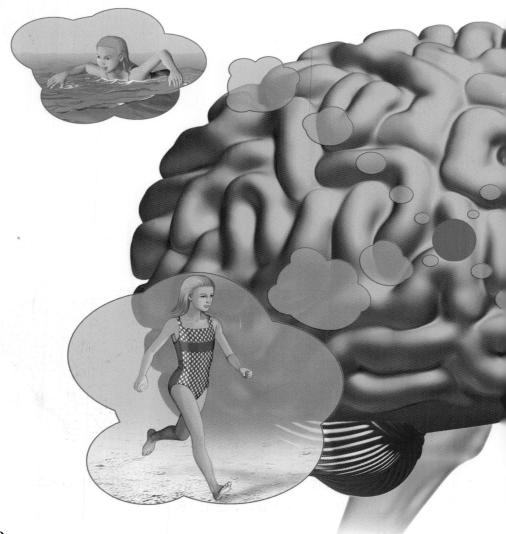

But she can also think of a new game!

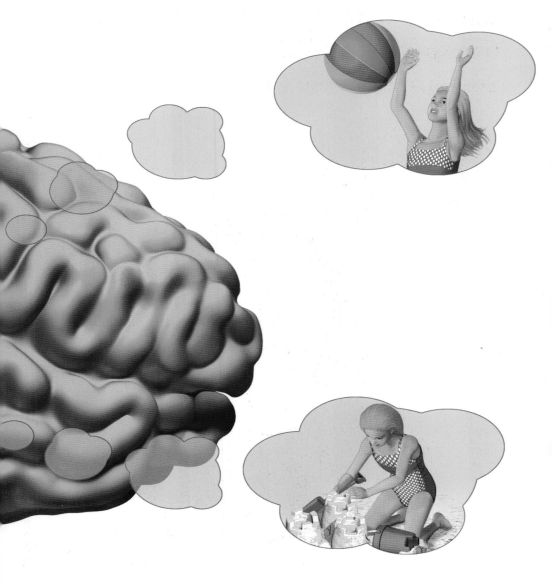

We use our brains to think and remember.
They also control our bodies.

Eyes to see

Harry sees things with his eyes.
Light goes into his eyes where it
turns into information for his brain.

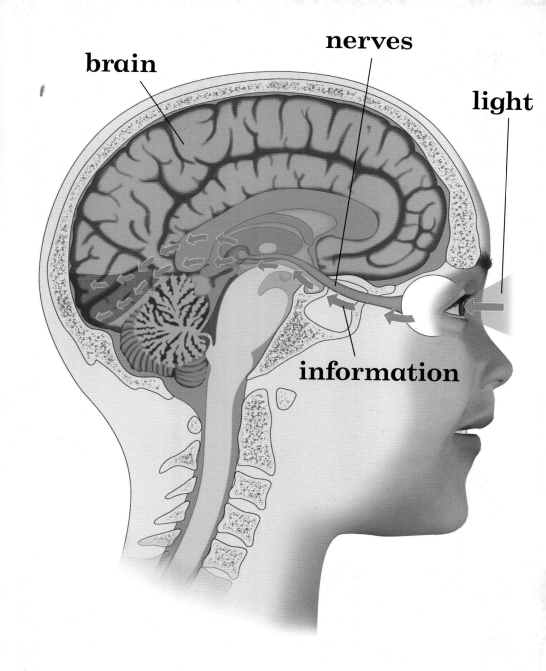

brain

nerves

light

information

Nerves carry information from Harry's eyes to his brain.

Ears to hear

Ella hears sounds with her ears.
Sounds go into her ears and move
the parts in them.

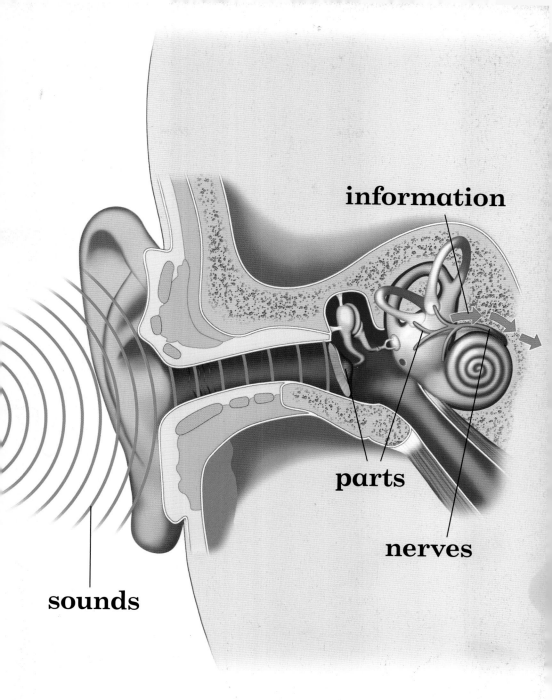

information

parts

nerves

sounds

The parts turn the sounds into information and nerves carry it to Ella's brain.

Food for energy

The energy to play this game comes from Harry and Ella's food.

Their bodies also get useful things, called nutrients, that they need from food.

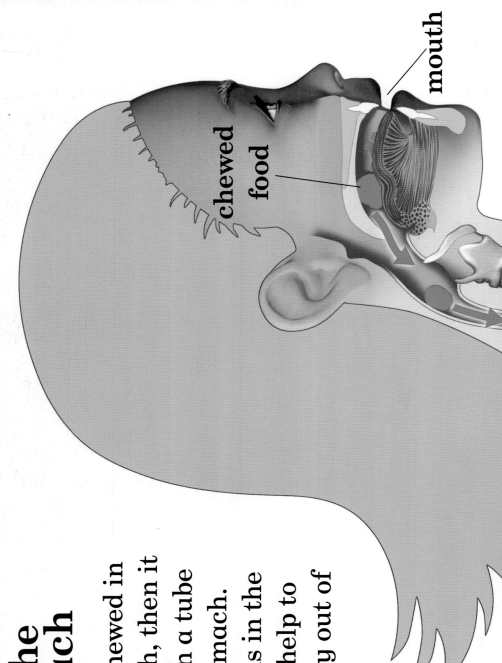

mouth

chewed food

Into the stomach

Food is chewed in the mouth, then it goes down a tube to the stomach. Chemicals in the stomach help to get energy out of the food.

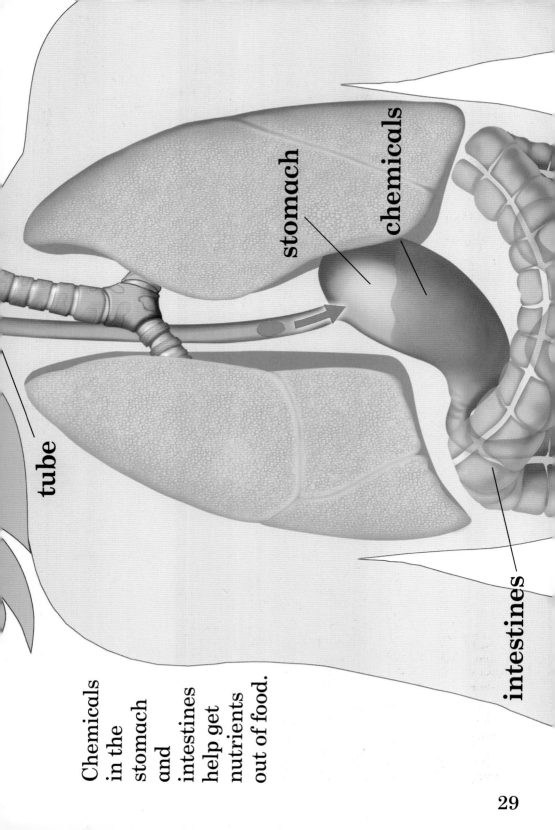

tube

stomach

chemicals

intestines

Chemicals in the stomach and intestines help get nutrients out of food.

29

In the intestines

Now the food moves from Ella and Harry's stomachs into their intestines.

Chemicals in their intestines get more useful nutrients from the food.

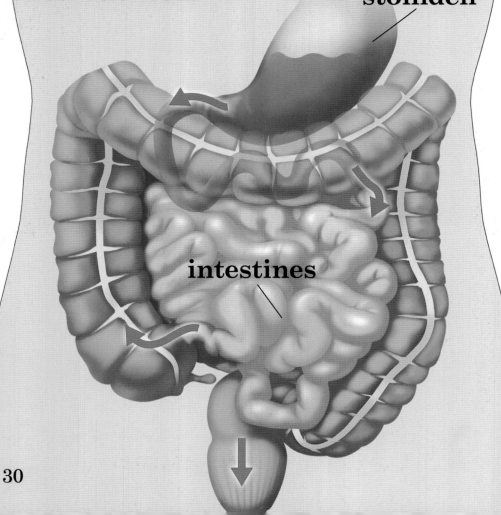

stomach

intestines

The nutrients go from the intestines and into the blood. This is done through blood vessels.

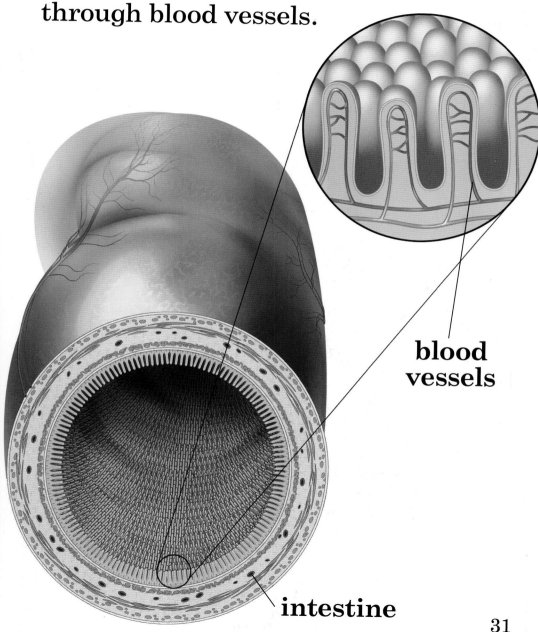

blood vessels

intestine

Breathing

Bodies need oxygen, a gas in the air. So Harry and Ella breathe in and out to get the oxygen.

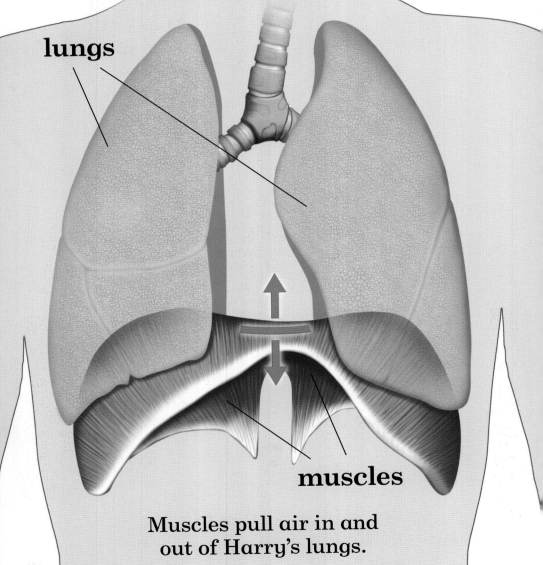

lungs

muscles

Muscles pull air in and out of Harry's lungs.

Oxygen gas goes from Harry and Ella's lungs into their blood.

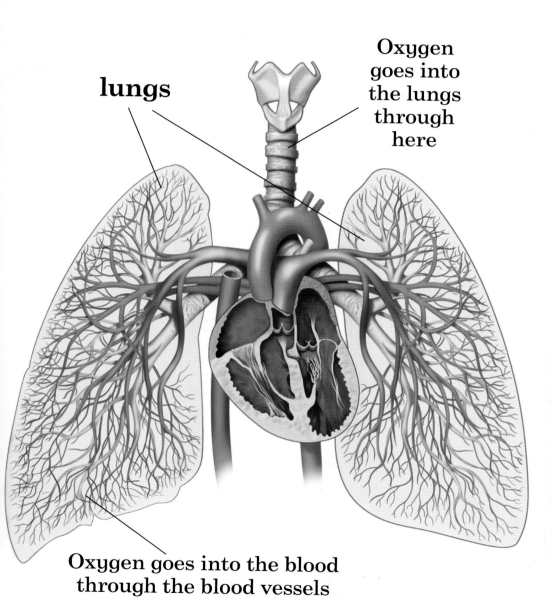

Oxygen
goes into
the lungs
through
here

lungs

Oxygen goes into the blood
through the blood vessels

Body pump

All the time, Harry and Ella's hearts pump blood around their bodies.

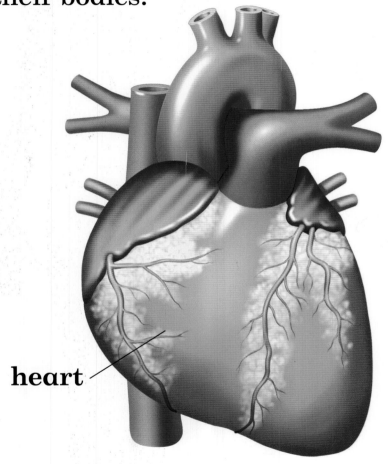

heart

A heart is made of muscle. It pumps blood right around the body and keeps going all the time.

Blood goes to
every part of the
body in little
tubes called
blood vessels.

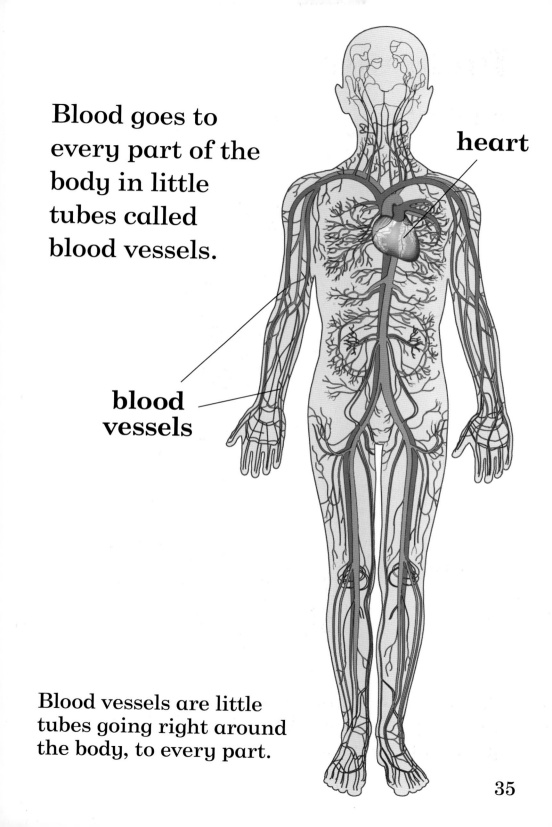

heart

blood
vessels

Blood vessels are little
tubes going right around
the body, to every part.

Busy blood

Blood vessels called arteries take blood with nutrients and energy from food to the muscles and all other parts of the body.

Arteries also carry blood around the body with oxygen from the lungs.

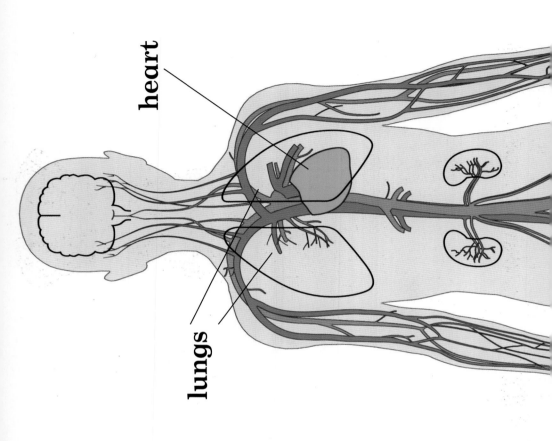

heart

lungs

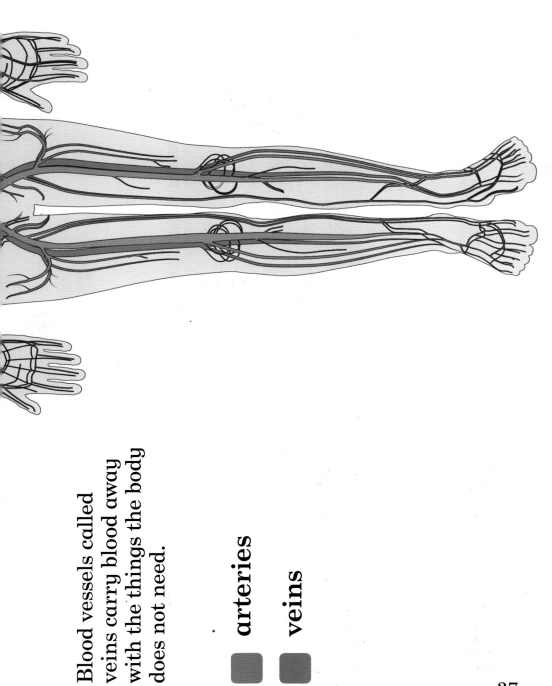

Blood vessels called
veins carry blood away
with the things the body
does not need.

█ arteries

█ veins

37

Go faster!

If Harry and Ella need more oxygen, they breathe faster and their hearts pump faster.

Muscles need more oxygen to work faster.

The brain makes the heart pump faster

The brain makes the lungs breathe faster

Stretchy skin

As Harry and Ella move, their stretchy skins keep the parts of their bodies together.

Heads, fingers and toes have have hair and nails as well as skin.

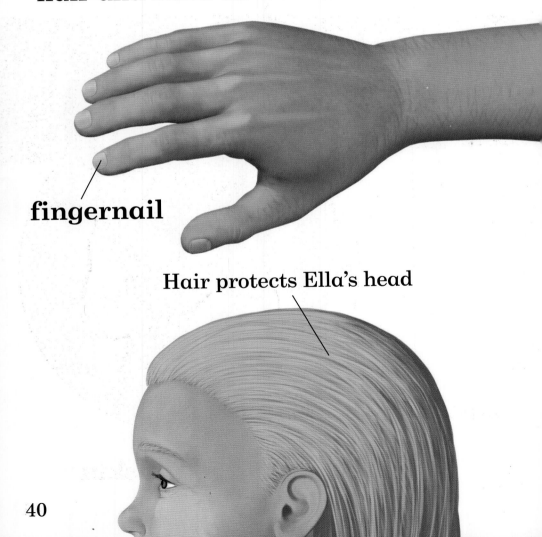

fingernail

Hair protects Ella's head

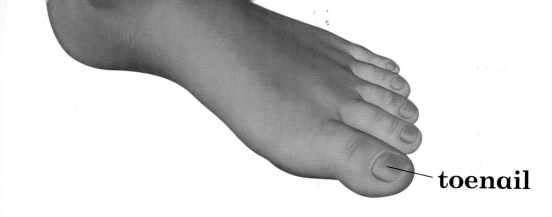

toenail

Nails protect Harry's fingers and toes.

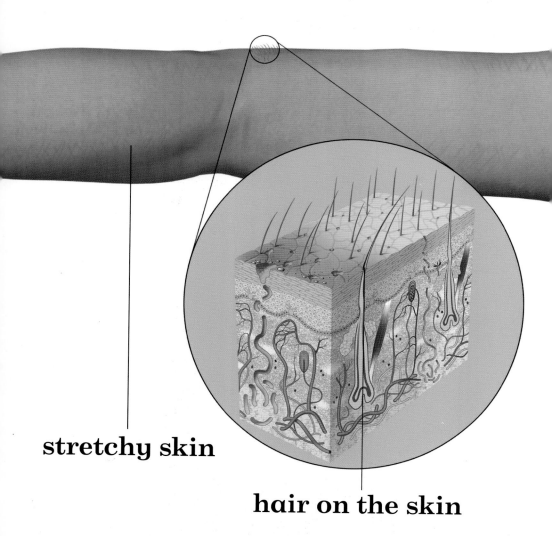

stretchy skin

hair on the skin

Time to sleep

Harry and Ella's amazing bodies and brains need rest to recover.

They go to sleep on the way back home!

Harry and Ella rest and recover as
they sleep on the way back home.

43

Picture glossary

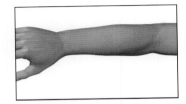 arm

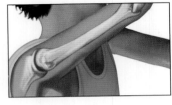 bones

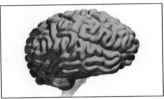 brain

 ear

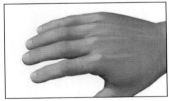 fingers

 hair

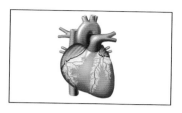 heart

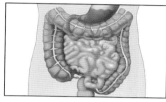 intestines

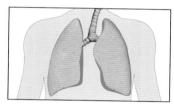 lungs

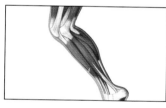 muscle

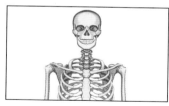 skeleton

 stomach

Index

The Human Body quiz

What have you learnt about the human body? Answer these questions and find out!

- Which parts of the body pull on the bones to make us move?

- Which parts carry orders from the brain to the rest of the body?

- Where does the energy for our bodies come from?

- Where does food go after the stomach?

- Which gas from the air do we breathe in to our lungs?

- What pumps blood all around the body?

Tick the books you've read!

Level 3

Puss in Boots — ☐
Sharks — ☐
Thumbelina — ☐
Aladdin — ☐
YOU won't like this present as much as I DO! — ☐

Jack and the Beanstalk — ☐
Rapunzel — ☐
The Jungle Book — ☐
Hansel and Gretel — ☐
The Elves and the Shoemaker — ☐

Harry and the Bucketful of Dinosaurs — ☐
The Red Knight — ☐
Planet Earth — ☐
Minibeasts — ☐
SNAKE ATTACK! — ☐

Level 4

Dick Whittington — ☐
Knights and Castles — ☐
Peter and the Wolf — ☐
Pinocchio — ☐
I am Inventing an INVENTION — ☐

The Pied Piper of Hamelin — ☐
Snow White and the Seven Dwarfs — ☐
The Wizard of Oz — ☐
The Little Mermaid — ☐
Alice in Wonderland — ☐

Harry and the Dinosaurs United — ☐
Heidi — ☐
Our Solar System — ☐
The Human Body — ☐
FRIENDS STICK TOGETHER — ☐